EXPLORER BOOKS

MAN-EATERS

by Lorraine Jean Hopping
and Christopher Egan

Published by The Trumpet Club
666 Fifth Avenue, New York, New York 10103

ISBN 0-440-84689-7

Printed in the United States of America
September 1992

1   3   5   7   9   10   8   6   4   2
CWO

PHOTOGRAPH CREDITS

p. 37: top, Animals Animals/© Carl Roessler; *bottom,* Animals Animals/©
Michael Dick. *p. 38:* Animals Animals/© Joyce Wilson. *p. 39: top,* Animals
Animals/© Len Rue, Jr.; *bottom,* © Gerry Ellis/The Wildlife Collection. *p. 40:*
top, © Gerry Ellis/The Wildlife Collection; *bottom,* Animals Animals/© Leonard
Lee Rue III. *p. 41: top,* © Gerry Ellis/The Wildlife Collection; *bottom,* Animals
Animals/© Len Clifford. *p. 42:* Animals Animals/© Leonard Lee Rue III. *p. 43:*
Animals Animals/© Karl Weidmann; *inset,* Photo/Nats/© Dr. Charles
Shipmetz, Jr. *p. 44:* Animals Animals/© Fritz Prenzel.

Cover: top, Animals Animals/© Zig Leszczynski;
bottom, R. Llewellyn/© SUPERSTOCK

To our parents—Bill and Marilyn Hopping
and Amy and Kevin Egan

Contents

Introduction

You've heard the stories. Sharks ripping surfers to shreds. Crocodiles lunging out of the water like meat-seeking missiles to snap at humans. Lions attacking African villagers . . .

Every year people report wild animal attacks on humans. But the truth is that very few humans die in the jaws or claws of animals. Surprisingly few animals are true man-eaters, animals that hunt, kill, and eat human flesh for their meals. Sharks are—but only some species. Saltwater crocodiles are. But probably not their cousins, the American alligators and crocodiles. Grizzlies and other big bears sometimes are. And lions, tigers, and other big cats living in the wild usually avoid us rather than eat us.

All of these animals are *predators,* or hunters. Predators must eat meat to survive. To do this, they must be in top form, in very good shape. Old and sick predators may starve to death because they are unable to hunt. Or they fall prey to other animals.

Predators usually follow four basic steps for hunting. They use keen senses to figure out when their *prey*—or animals they hunt for food—is nearby.

They decide whether or not to attack, depending on what their chances of success are. Predators don't want to get hurt. So they usually attack only if all the odds are in their favor.

Once they decide to go for it, predators must find a way to catch their prey. Some, like lions, stalk their prey. *Stalkers* stalk because they are slower than their prey. Their strategy is to stay hidden during the hunt so that they can get as close as possible before pouncing. Some hide behind rocks and trees. Some animals' coloring allows them to blend in with their natural surroundings. This is called *camouflage.*

Sharks chase their prey. *Chasers* chase because they can often outrun (or outswim) their prey. Bears are both stalkers and chasers. They may stalk their prey, creeping up on unsuspecting animals, and then chase the prey once they're close enough to pounce. Lions sometimes combine stalking, chasing, and pouncing as well. Some predators, like crocodiles, *ambush,* or lie in wait for, their prey, attacking by surprise once prey comes to them.

Finally predators need to kill the prey, or at least make it weak enough so that it can't fight back. To kill, predators need weapons, such as teeth and claws. A bear delivers a blow to its prey with a mighty paw. Some sharks bite with their sharp teeth. Sharks are born knowing how to kill their prey. But cats learn this behavior from their mothers. As cubs they tend to play with prey, batting at other animals with their paws. Killing is a lesson cubs must learn for survival.

Like all animals, humans are meat. So why are

feeding attacks on people rare? After all, predators like lions and bears and crocodiles are often bigger and stronger than we are.

One reason may be that humans are the world's most feared and successful predator! Like all hunters, we have weapons for making the kill. And our most deadly one—brainpower—has given us killer tools such as high-powered rifles. These high-tech weapons are no match for even the biggest and strongest beasts.

When predators *do* attack humans, it may be because they have no choice, not always because they're hungry. They're sick or old, cornered, scared, defending their territory, or protecting their young. So even though they're up against a smarter, better-equipped enemy, they risk their lives to attack in self-defense.

In fact, we're so much better at killing that we're killing off the predators. We've taken over many of their *habitats,* or homelands. We've hunted them and the animals they depend on for food. We've made life so tough that great white sharks, Siberian tigers, grizzly bears, alligators, Asiatic lions, Bengal tigers, and other large predators may be in danger of dying out. Predators reproduce slowly. Unless we protect them, they often can't replace the ones that we've wiped out.

What would the world be like without predators? Think about their prey, animals like seals, rabbits, deer, and zebras. Predators usually hunt the weakest, sickest, and oldest of these animals. They're easier to catch and kill. Without predators, these weaker animals could survive. And that would keep whole populations of these animals from growing stronger.

Also, without predators to thin the ranks, prey populations could reproduce out of control. (Most prey populations reproduce much more rapidly than predators do.) Soon, there would be too many of them. They wouldn't have enough food to eat or land to live on. Many of them would starve to death.

Plus, don't forget the *scavengers*—bald eagles, vultures, hyenas, and others. These animals feed on dead flesh. They depend on predators to leave behind some of their kill. The fewer predators there are, the fewer leftovers for scavengers there may be.

So a world without predators would be a world in trouble! Want the truth? Here are the *real* stories behind these so-called "man-eating" beasts. Many of these animals make people fear for their lives. And people should indeed be wary of them. But most of them would rather steer clear of a human being if given the choice. Some would rather die than eat you! Read all about these amazing animals—and learn how to stay safe if you happen to cross their paths.

1

Meet the Real "Jaws"

The date was September 13, 1988, hurricane season on the Atlantic Coast. One storm, Hurricane Florence, had slammed into the Gulf of Mexico days before. Hurricane Gilbert, one of the worst in this century, was on its way. But the day *before* Gilbert arrived, the weather in the Gulf couldn't have been more inviting. It was so pleasant that three friends decided to go swimming.

Susan Barnes, Terry Segrest, and Jon Martin anchored their boat in a state park near Panama City, Florida. They dove into murky waters just 40 miles away from the place where *Jaws 2* had been filmed. The infamous killer shark of the *Jaws* movies was much on their minds. So much so, that when Susan and Terry spotted porpoises, they hopped back into the boat.

Jon teased his friends by humming the scary *Jaws* theme—da-da, da-da, da-da. . . . He rocked the boat, just like the fictional killer shark. Then his body jerked. "Help me!" he shouted.

At first, Susan thought Jon was still teasing. Then she spotted a dark shape larger than a man. A *real*

"Jaws"! Jon beat the shark with his hands. His hands were quickly shredded by the shark's sandpaper-like skin. In a bloody tug-of-war, Susan and Terry tried to pull Jon onto the boat. The shark bit a chunk out of his lower leg and then circled around for another attack. This time, its teeth ripped into Jon's thigh.

By the time rescuers pulled Jon onto the beach minutes later, he was dead. As they did so, two other sharks cruised nearby.

There's no question about it, some sharks *do* eat people. But attacks are very rare. And deaths like Jon's are even rarer. The International Shark Attack File is a list of all attacks around the world that witnesses report. Scientist George Burgess maintains the file at the Florida Museum of Natural History in Gainesville. He estimates fifty to seventy-five people fall victim to shark attacks each year. Of these, five to ten victims die.

However, many attacks are never reported—especially those in South America, Africa, and Asia. Sharks swim in waters all over the world. Most live in the open ocean, preferring warm waters to cold. However, when the weather becomes too warm, sharks will migrate long distances to reach cooler waters.

Some sharks, like the *great white,* live far out at sea in deep tropical waters, but feed on seals in shallow waters close to shore. *Lemon sharks* live in the Atlantic Ocean, close to shore, near reefs. Though sharks are saltwater fish, some sharks, like the *bull shark,* somehow manage to make their way up fresh-water rivers from the Indian, Pacific, and Atlantic Oceans.

Of course, if you don't swim in or near ocean waters, your chances of being shark bait are zero. If you do decide to risk it, remember that your chances of being struck by lightning are about thirty times greater than of being bitten by a shark! Most shark attacks in the United States happen off the Atlantic Coast. The second largest number of attacks occur in the Pacific Ocean, off the California Coast.

There are about 350 kinds of sharks—all of which are officially classified as fish. A fish is any cold-blooded *vertebrate,* or animal with a backbone, that lives in the water, has fins, and breathes through gills. Only 39 kinds of sharks are known to have attacked people. The biggest shark, the *whale shark,* is harmless. It lives near the surface in tropical waters and feeds on the tiniest plants and animals—simple-celled organisms called *plankton.*

Other kinds of sharks are just as harmless. Biologist Carol Roden recalls flying over beaches in northern Florida in 1989. From the air, she spotted hundreds of large sharks swimming near a sandbar —side-by-side with humans! Shark expert Eugenie Clark likes to study her subjects up close. She sometimes pets them and even hitches rides from them!

Which sharks *aren't* good swimming pals? The great white, which starred in the *Jaws* movies, is the top people killer. It can grow to 18 feet long—about the length of four 13-year-olds lying head to toe! Even Eugenie Clark stays in a metal cage while she observes great whites.

George Burgess believes a *tiger shark* (found in tropical and subtropical oceans) may have killed Jon Martin. In addition to the great white and the tiger shark, these sharks round out the "10 Most Dangerous" list: bulls, *makos* (all oceans), *whitetips* (all tropical seas and oceans), lemons, *hammerheads* (shallow tropical and subtropical waters), *gray nurses* (shallow tropical waters, near reefs), *sand sharks* (warm ocean waters), and *dusky sharks* (off the west coast of Africa).

It's Time for Dinner

Why do some sharks attack people? They certainly don't do it out of anger or revenge, like the *Jaws* villain. Like all predators, sharks eat meat to live. And on very rare occasions, they may hunt humans for meat. They may also attack when they feel threatened or mistake people for other kinds of prey.

Sharks have keen senses to locate and compete for their prey. Suppose a possible meal is swimming a mile or so from a great white shark. The shark can't see it. But it can probably hear it.

As prey thrashes around, it creates vibrations. Sound vibrations travel faster through water than air. And they travel outward, like ripples on a pond.

Sharks tune in especially well to low, uneven sounds. These are the sounds of an animal in trouble—an easy-to-catch animal in trouble. (Or they're the sounds of shark hunters who know how to increase their catch! Shark fishermen often tap on the boat to lure sharks.) When Jon Martin hummed the *Jaws* theme, knocked on the boat, and thrashed around, he may have unknowingly attracted his killer.

As the shark swims closer, other senses spring into action. Water carries odors, just as air does. The odor-filled water constantly enters one side of the shark's nostril and flows out the other. Lemon sharks may be able to smell as little as 10 drops of tuna extract in water equal to an average-size swimming pool. Some reef sharks can detect 1 drop in a quarter-acre of water more than 6 feet deep!

The smell of blood is, of course, especially attractive to a shark. It means other predators have found a meal and there may be leftovers. Or it means an animal is wounded.

So the shark zigzags closer, picking up more signals, odors, or other evidence. Or, it may just make a beeline for the blood.

The prey soon comes into view. Shark eyes have reflectors, which act like mirrors. The reflectors bounce light back into the eye for better vision in dark or murky waters. (That's why shark eyes, like cat eyes, shine in the dark.)

Even so, ocean water can be too murky to see through clearly. Just days before the attack on Jon Martin and his friends in Panama City, Hurricane Florence stirred up the Gulf waters. Swimmers could only see about 5 feet in front of them. In these conditions, sharks may mistake humans for other, more commonly eaten animals. A surfer paddling on a surfboard may look like a seal, for instance.

Sharks also use their sense of touch. They can feel water movements, just as you can feel a gust of air from a passing car. The movements register on a string of nerves from snout to tail. The nerves are called the *lateral line*. (Most fish have one.)

At very close range, a "sixth sense" comes into play. Unlike animals on land, sharks can detect tiny electric currents. All living creatures give off electricity! How? A beating heart, the swish of a tail, water passing over gills—all these muscle actions create electric currents. Nerve cells on the shark's snout pick up these electric signals. This sense allows sharks to attack prey that they can't see, hear, smell, or feel. For example, hammerhead sharks can scan the ocean floor like metal detectors, searching for stingrays buried in mud.

To Bite or Not To Bite?

Next, the shark has to decide whether or not to attack. Some sharks, like great whites, might bite first and ask questions later. It's their way of sampling the prey to see if it tastes good. It also weakens an animal, making the final kill easier and less risky.

Diver Rodney Fox was a victim of a well-known great white attack in 1963. He never saw the shark until its giant jaws clamped down on his chest. Rodney punched the shark in the eye and tried to claw the eye out of its socket. But the creature attacked again. This time, it grabbed the fish bait around Rodney's belt and dragged the diver down. Somehow, he freed himself and floated to the surface. A 4-hour operation and 462 stitches just barely saved his life.

More often, sharks circle their prey before attacking. Like most predators, they're cautious. They prefer to size up a situation before wasting energy on a tough kill. Sharks may even brush up against an animal with their snout before biting.

Half an hour after the Panama City attack, divers anchored in the same area. They didn't know what had just happened to Jon Martin. One felt something brush against his leg. As he looked down, he saw a shark snag his flipper. He quickly jumped to safety in the boat.

Lots of blood and animal parts in the water can attract dozens of sharks. That's when they're likely to go into a feeding frenzy. As all these sharks compete to eat the food, they don't have time to circle around and check things out. So they crazily snap at everything in range—including fellow sharks! The frenzied motions may help them tear apart the prey.

To make a kill, sharks need weapons. Sharks have speed. They power. And they have teeth.

Sharks can outswim most of their prey—including humans. Studies have shown some types reach speeds of up to 22 to 43 miles per hour. Such speeds can only be maintained for short periods. These are only estimates, however, and only for short bursts!

The jaw power of a great white creates about 20 tons of pressure per square inch of flesh. That's like three very large elephants standing on your thumb! Just before the shark clamps down, its loose jaw moves forward and the snout moves back. Rows and rows of sharp teeth are exposed.

Teeth may be its deadliest weapons. Sharks generally have four to six rows of them. Some have as many as twenty rows. The front-row teeth stand straight up and may break off during an attack. Within 24 hours, the next tooth in line rises up and takes its place. One tiger shark may grow 24,000 teeth over a 10-year period!

Each kind of shark has unique teeth depending on how it kills its prey. Tiger sharks have teeth with saw-like edges. Great whites do, too, but their teeth are shaped like triangles. The pointy bottoms are better for slicing and tearing through tough skin. Sand sharks spike their prey with teeth that look like deadly golf tees. Hammerhead shark teeth are angled and jagged, so they grip better when prey tries to get away.

Newborn sharks have a full set of teeth, and are ready to hunt for prey at birth. This makes sharks sound like fierce predators. But the truth is, sharks have much more to fear from us than we do from them. Just consider the numbers. Usually sharks kill fewer than ten people each year. But we slaughter *hundreds of thousands* of them. Shark fin soup is especially popular in Asia. Trophy hunters like to display shark jaws over their mantle. And shark "steak" has become fashionable at some restaurants. What are the shark's chances against such human predators?

2

Never Smile at a Crocodile

American tourist Ginger Meadows wanted to have as much fun as possible during her visit to Australia in March of 1987. She especially wanted to enjoy the great outdoors. So she and some friends decided to explore a waterfall on the Prince Regent River.

It would be an adventure, they thought, climbing rock ledges and swimming in the falls. But as they set out for the top, Ginger and her friend Jane Burchett changed their minds. The rocks were too steep and slippery. So instead, they dove into the water below.

There, they could swim without danger of falling. In fact, danger was the last thing on Ginger's mind. She probably never expected to hear a voice shouting from the top of the falls . . .

"Crocodile! Get out of the water!"

Ginger and Jane turned and saw a long, dark shape below the water. They froze with terror. A crocodile was floating, quietly, no more than 10 yards away. Its yellow eyes were locked on the two human intruders.

Jane screamed and threw a shoe at the giant reptile. The crocodile froze, but just for a split second. Ginger decided to make a break for it. She dove away from the beast and headed for dry land. She never had a chance. The crocodile lunged with a few strokes of its powerful tail and seized Ginger in its jaws. Jane and the others watched, horrified.

The reptile yanked Ginger below the water. Her friends climbed down the cliff, jumped into their boat, and made loud noises to scare the crocodile. A short time later, the crocodile resurfaced with Ginger's body in its mouth. It submerged and disappeared, taking its human prey with it.

Like sharks, some crocodiles have killed people. But not very often. Ginger Meadows was one of only three known crocodile victims in Australia in 1987. From 1975 to 1988, saltwater crocodiles are reported to have killed twelve people in that country. (Attacks in Africa, India, and other countries often aren't reported, so exact numbers are impossible to come by.)

Crocodile attacks in Australia may be rare. But they *are* on the rise. The animals were once *endangered,* or dying out. But they have been protected from human hunting since the early 1970s, so their numbers have increased. That fact, along with a rise in tourism, has brought people and crocodiles together like never before.

But not all crocodiles are big or fierce enough to ambush people. Crocodiles are giant lizard-like *vertebrates,* or animals with backbones. They have large jaws and narrow snouts with sharp, pointy teeth. Their long, powerful tails help propel them through the water and up out of the water. The back and sides of their long bodies are covered with thick scales or horny plates. They have four short legs and webbed feet that allow them to swim or crawl on land. Their main habitats are southern Florida, the West Indian islands of the Caribbean, parts of Central and South America, and northern Australia.

They spend most of their time either in the water cooling off or in the sun warming up their bodies. This is because all crocodiles are reptiles. And reptiles are cold-blooded. Cold-blooded creatures have body temperatures that change depending on the temperature of their surroundings.

When crocodiles go underwater, their nostrils and ears close, and a transparent "third eyelid" protects their eyes without hurting their vision. They can also feed while under the water, without swallowing water and drowning. They usually do their sleeping in the water, too.

One thing a crocodile does on land is lay its eggs. Crocodile eggs look like hen's eggs, but are longer and have a less-brittle shell. Crocodiles conceal their eggs in nests of rubbish and vegetation, or they bury them in sandy beaches. The female of some types guards the nest until the young are hatched. Heat from the sun or from the decomposition of the nest material promotes rapid development of the eggs. When she can hear the young reptiles grunting, the female digs them out of the nest. Some crocodiles help their young hatch and then carry them in their mouth to the water. Soon after hatching, the young are ready to fend for themselves. Crocodiles grow rapidly until they reach maturity.

There are twelve species of crocodiles, but only two species are known to eat humans. One man-eater is the *saltwater crocodile,* or "saltie." The name is tricky because this crocodile lives in salty *and* fresh waters in India, southern Asia, and northern Australia. A saltie is the prime suspect in the Ginger Meadows case. Mostly the bigger ones—they can grow up to 18 feet long—attack humans. (The bigger the crocodile, the older it is. They just keep growing until they die.) However, smaller crocodiles that are about 5 or 6 feet long can attack humans, especially injured people and small children.

The *Nile crocodile* is the number-one four-legged killer in Africa—of beasts *and* humans! It outkills African lions, leopards, buffaloes, hippos, hyenas, rhinos, and elephants put together! Ancient Egyptians, who lived along the crocodile-infested Nile River, believed these animals were sacred. They worshipped a crocodile god named Sobek.

Why are Nile crocodiles and salties so fearsome and bloodthirsty? They have to be, if they want to eat and not be eaten. As they grow up, these species have more enemies (humans and sharks, for instance) than any other crocodile, so they have to compete harder for food. They'll eat just about anything of any size—fish, snakes, leopards, turtles, antelope, birds, zebras . . . and sometimes humans.

The Ultimate Ambush Animal

What's it like to make a killing? Suppose you're an Australian saltie. Sprout yourself a powerful tail, grow two to three times taller than you are, and get down on all fours.

If it's daytime, the saltie will spend hours lying on shore, warming up in the sun. Doing not much of anything is a popular pastime for reptiles.

Because a saltie is so sluggish, it doesn't need much food energy to keep its body going, so it doesn't eat very often. Days or weeks may pass between meals.

Suppose today the saltie's sharp ears hear something splashing that wasn't splashing before. Or maybe it spots a thirsty animal at the water's edge. The saltie watches the animal patiently to see if it looks harmful.

Satisfied that this is an easy target, the saltie silently slips into the water. Like a submarine, it can sink and resurface at will. And it can hover just below the surface. Its eyes and nostrils are on top of its head. Like periscopes and snorkles, they allow the saltie to see and breathe even when it's hidden under the water.

Safely out of sight, it waits, as still as a log. What is it waiting for? It has to be absolutely, positively sure this meal will be captured in a snap. Its life depends on it. Why? Unlike sharks, the saltie is an ambush animal. Its best weapon is a surprise attack. If the prey knows the saltie is there, the saltie will have to battle hard to catch it. And the saltie tires quickly—that would make the saltie an easy meal for a shark or other hungry hunter!

Luckily for the saltie, today's prey is busy drinking. The saltie closes in. It drifts toward the target, always watching. The saltie's dark coloring camouflages its body well. And the saltie can stay perfectly still underwater for over an hour if it has to. As it waits, its heart slows down to one beat every three minutes.

As soon as all the advantages are on the saltie's side, it's time to attack. . . .

Meat-seeking Missiles

Crocodiles are modern relatives of dinosaurs. They belong to the same group of reptiles, called *archosaurs,* that were the ancestors of dinosaurs *and* birds. Maybe that's why they can lunge into the air!

Crocodiles launch themselves out of the water like meat-seeking missiles. Even big ones are capable of vaulting 5 or 6 feet straight up out of the water to snap at birds. Or they can snap sideways under the water to capture a fish.

Sometimes, they rush forward onto a beach, lunging at prey. Adults can dash across land for several yards, either at a gallop or on their bellies.

To make the kill, crocodiles use several weapons and strategies. A favorite trick is to grab a target by the nose with their sharp, pointy teeth and not let go. Or they may deliver sledgehammer blows with their snouts or tails. Sometimes, crocodiles seize the prey in their jaws and drag it underwater. Even big mammals—like zebras—have drowned this way. Sure, zebras can outrun crocodiles on land, but if the zebra or any animal gets too close to the water's edge, it may be in trouble. The crocodile's strike is lightning-quick, and it can grab on to any part of the animal's body. When this happens, the extremely strong crocodile can haul the animal into the water.

If the meal is *really* big, a crocodile may roll over and over in the water with its victim. This tactic is called the "death roll." The violent movements help crocodiles confuse prey while at the same time tearing away large chunks of flesh. Needless to say, it almost always helps the crocodile win a tough struggle.

Just ask Australian adventurer Val Plumwood. She's spent a lot of time in the wilderness in an ongoing effort to protect animals. But she barely survived three death rolls during a crocodile attack in 1985.

Val was in a canoe. She saw a crocodile moving toward her. The crocodile tried to cut Val off, tipping the canoe over and spilling her into the water. Val tried repeatedly to pull herself up out of the water by low-hanging branches, but several times she was pulled back in as the crocodile rolled over again and again. Later she commented, "I'd rather go through anything than one of those rolls. . . . By the end of the third roll, I thought I'd really had it. I was thinking, 'I wish it would finish me off quickly.' "

The crocodile tends to hold its prey underwater to drown it. It then rips chunks of flesh off the victim's body. This ripping motion is often violent and messy, more so than with other predators, and uneaten body parts have been found strewn around attack sites. Although crocodiles may defend their own kills, it is not uncommon for a group of crocodiles to feed on a single large victim.

Like sharks, crocodiles can replace teeth that may break off during an attack. Their teeth aren't built for chewing. So sometimes they have to hide large prey in water until it begins to rot and becomes soft enough to swallow.

Crocodiles defending this hidden food can be especially tough. Like many predators, they're territorial. They stake out an area and call it their own. They have to, in order to make sure they have a steady food supply.

3

Lions and Tigers and . . . Pounce!

"We never before gave a second thought to a mountain lion being a dangerous animal," said Mike Aderhold of the Montana Department of Fish and Wildlife. "But the events of this past summer have changed that."

The "events" were not pretty. On July 23, 1989, a 9-year-old boy and his friends met a 40-pound *mountain lion* in Glacier National Park, Montana. The kids outnumbered and even outweighed the cat. Most predators don't attack prey that is bigger and heavier than they are—or that is well-protected by a group or herd. But the mountain lion still managed to bite the boy on his head and neck. His parents rushed to the scene and scared away the hungry mountain lion. It later died by gunshot. The injured boy survived.

Two months later, a 5-year-old boy was playing near his trailer home in Missoula, Montana, when a mountain lion attacked and killed him. It was the first proven death of its kind in that state.

Vancouver Island, Canada, has had at least thirteen major attacks since 1953. In 1985 three girls hiked along a well-worn trail. They unknowingly walked right up to a mountain lion. Predator and prey stared at each other for a moment. Then the girls screamed and ran. Alyson Parker, 10, tripped. As the big cat pounced on her, the friends ran back to camp for help. Counselor Lila Lifely drove the cat away by beating it with her first aid kit. Alyson survived after receiving 200 stitches in her head.

Despite these accidents, the fact is that mountain lions very rarely attack humans of any age. Records list less than 100 proven cases in the past few centuries. But when they do attack, these smallish cats go after smallish people—children. Children tend to look and act more like prey than do adults. And running away—as the three girls did—can trigger an attack from almost any predator. So can appearing weak and scared—as Alyson did when she fell.

Mountain lions are also called *cougars* and *pumas.* They live on the North American continent, mainly in the U.S. and Canadian Rocky mountain areas. They're one of several types of big cats.

All big cats are carnivores and hunters. Which ones are big enough to hunt humans? *Jaguars* are spotted cats that live mainly in South America. *Leopards* are spotted, too, but they live mostly in Asia and Africa. Leopards that look black are sometimes called *panthers.* The black coat makes the spots underneath hard to see, but you can see them if you get close. *Cheetahs* are also spotted. And these superfast sprinters live in Africa.

The truth is, all of these big cats tend to shy away from humans. Two of the biggest cats—*lions* and *tigers*—usually do too. But not always.

Bengal tigers live mainly in India. One of the biggest populations is in a park area called the Sundarban Forest. Laws protecting the tigers have caused their numbers to increase. At the same time, more honey gatherers, fishermen, and other workers are now using the park. The combination can—on rare occasions—be deadly. As honey gatherers pick through the thick forest, they sometimes disturb sleeping tigers while searching for bees. Tigers attack the honey gatherers in self-defense.

Hungry tigers will eat fish caught in man-made nets. Sometimes, fishermen come across these swimming tigers by accident. Without rifles or knives, they are unable to defend themselves against these powerful predators. Once tigers attack and kill an animal (including a human), their instincts tell them to "eat it." Park officials of the Sundarban Forest report about twenty to forty deaths per year caused by tigers.

During the day, a tiger usually remains hidden in the forest. It comes out in the evening to stalk its prey. It waits for its victims by forest paths and along river banks. A tiger eats many different kinds of animals—ox, wild boar, deer, peacock—and it also fishes with its paws. Tigers also eat tortoises and other reptiles.

If the prey is too large to be eaten at a single meal, the tiger drags it away and hides it in the trees. The tiger returns to eat the meat for the next few days, even if it goes bad. (Leopards and lions don't eat rotten meat.) If they are hunting near villages, tigers sometimes raid herds of farm animals.

Tigers prefer not to attack once the prey knows

they're there. Park officials in India use this fact to protect workers. They pass out rubber masks painted with big-eyed faces. Workers now wear the masks on the *backs* of their heads. That way, tigers think the people can spot them from all angles, and they don't risk an attack. The beady-eyed masks work well. Once a worker took his off to eat lunch, and a tiger pounced on him!

Master Stalkers

The most famous lion attacks happened near Tsavo, Kenya, in Africa almost a century ago. In 1898–99 workers were building a railroad straight through lion country. A pair of the big cats polished off dozens of the workers one by one, often at night while the men slept. It took two years to track and kill these "man-eaters of Tsavo," as they became known.

Why did these lions develop a taste for human flesh? Maybe the workers were easy prey. As they spread out along the railway, they couldn't defend themselves well. And neither could the people sent out to bury the dead. They were scared of the lions, so they quickly dropped their human corpses and fled. Not being ones to pass up a free meal, the lions feasted on the human flesh. And when they didn't find any more dead human flesh, they soon came to catch and kill live people.

Fortunately, most African lions are not as aggressive as the Tsavo lions. What do African lions *usually* eat? Gazelles, zebras, wildebeests (large, grazing animals that are also called gnus), and whatever else they can catch on the open plains or at the local water hole.

To understand how African lions locate food, it is important to understand how they live. African lions live in *prides,* or families—a single male, one or more females, and their cubs. One purpose of the pride is to keep other lions out of its territory. Too many lions in one area will wipe out available prey.

Males usually protect the cubs at home while the lionesses do the hunting. Females make 85 to 90 percent of all kills. The males are usually allowed to eat their fill of the kill first, even though the females make the kill. Why? It may be a simple matter of size —male lions weigh about 400 pounds, while females weigh about 250 pounds—the large males may overpower the smaller females. Or maybe the males eat first because they patrol the pride area, protecting lionesses while they are bearing their young, two or three cubs at a time. No one knows for sure. The cubs eat last.

Lionesses may walk 25 to 30 miles in a single outing to find their food! Sometimes, lionesses get lucky and stumble on a sleeping meal, such as a porcupine, by accident. Or they dig animals such as rabbits out of their burrows. (House cats like to do this, too.) They may even ambush their prey at water holes or along popular trails. From time to time, lions and lionesses may hunt together. Two lions fan out and chase their targets into the waiting jaws of family members.

But the lionesses' main strategy is to stalk their food. One reason they often hunt at night is so that the prey can't see them while they're stalking. Like shark eyes, cat eyes have reflectors to make night vision easier.

Like the crocodile, a stalking lioness is cautious and patient. She waits until she has the advantage. And she prefers the surprise attack—pouncing on an animal that has no idea it's being watched.

The lioness knows by experience that she has to sneak within one or two leaps of her target—maybe 10 or 20 yards. Otherwise, almost any prey with four healthy legs can outrun her. She can charge at about 35 miles per hour at best. But she can't keep up that speed for long. Meanwhile, prey such as the giraffe can run 37 miles per hour; the ostrich, 43.5 miles per hour; and the Thomson's gazelle, 50 miles per hour. (In comparison, cheetahs run 71 miles per hour. They are the only cats that are much faster than their prey. The world's fastest humans can run only 23 miles per hour.)

To sneak really close, the lioness uses almost anything for cover—long grass, rocks, trees. Her sleek, trim body is hard to spot. Color camouflage helps, too. The tawny-colored lioness blends in with the dry grassland. (Tiger stripes, leopard spots, and other markings help these cats hide in shady forests.)

A big male with a fluffy mane, on the other hand, can't hide as easily. His mane makes him look like a moving haystack in a field of grass! This may be one reason why females hunt more often than males.

The stalking lioness crouches low and never takes her eyes off the target. If the prey lifts its head, the cat freezes—paw in midair if need be. As soon as the victim lowers its head to feed, the lioness steps quietly on her padded feet. Cat claws, except for cheetahs', retract, or pull back, so that the stalker makes less noise. (The claws of dogs and bears stay put. These animals don't usually stalk when they hunt.)

What happens if the prey gets a whiff of the lioness? Or spots her moving? She'll sit up and relax as if she was never interested in the first place. You may have seen a house cat do this, too.

Pouncing Power

A pouncing lioness is one big ball of tightly wound muscle. She crouches, tenses, quivers, and then explodes off her powerful back legs. Only about one out of five leaps hits its mark and sticks. (Lions get better odds with group hunting.)

Sometimes, gazelles "spronk" to safety. *Spronking* is a *defense strategy,* or something the prey does to protect itself. It means they bounce high up and then come down with all four hooves hitting the ground at once. They usually spronk in a wild, zigzag pattern. Wildebeests defend themselves by bunching together and forming a fortress-like wall. Some animals circle the lions to confuse them.

Of course, sometimes the lioness does manage to hold on with her gripping claws. She almost always keeps at least two feet on the ground during an attack. That way, she can more easily drag her victim to the ground.

Then it's time for her other deadly weapon: a bite to the throat. All cats have four "killer" canines—two front teeth on top and two on bottom for biting and ripping flesh. Killing prey quickly isn't easy, and it doesn't come naturally. Mothers have to teach their cubs how to do it. They show their young how to bite down on the back of the neck or the throat, sometimes slicing the animal's jugular vein (in the neck) in half. Most victims die within minutes. (Well-fed house cats may not know how to kill properly. That may explain why they bring home live, but mangled, mice or other prey.)

Lions sometimes eat the inner organs first. Then they dine on the flesh, working their way to the head. A 400-pound male lion can eat one-fourth of its body weight in a sitting. That's like an 80-pound kid eating a 20-pound steak for dinner!

Big Cats in Trouble

African lions and cheetahs, Indian tigers, North American cougars, and South American jaguars are endangered. When humans take over their lands and turn them into farms, they hunt the big cats out of fear or for sport. And they compete for the same food —deer, elk, antelope, and sheep in North America.

In the 1700s cougars roamed throughout North America. In fact, the first reported attack on a human happened in the eastern state of Pennsylvania in 1751. Now, mountain lions are rarely spotted in just eleven western states and two Canadian provinces. And in some areas, populations of wild grazing animals, which the mountain lions have traditionally preyed on, have grown out of control.

For example, consider what happened in the Kaibab Indian Reservation in Arizona from 1920 to 1940. The population of mule deer jumped from 4,000 to 100,000 in just eighteen years. Why? Because their natural predator, the mountain lion, quickly started disappearing. Hunters killed off the cougars without considering the consequences. As a result, the mule deer didn't have enough food to go around. They destroyed the grasslands by overgrazing. So a lot of them starved to death.

Without big cats, prey populations aren't the only animals that are affected. Scavengers are affected, too. Even with their healthy appetites, all big cats usually leave plenty of leftovers. Scavenger animals —hyenas in Africa, coyotes in North America, vultures just about everywhere—depend on big cats' kill for their meals.

Mountain lions, tigers, lions, and other big cats can be dangerous. But if humans continue to kill off these important predators in the food chain, we are endangering the delicate balance of the ecosystem.

4

Beware the Bears

Two friends—Ted Moore and Roger May—camped near Yellowstone National Park (in northwestern Wyoming, Montana, and Idaho) on June 24, 1983. That night, they ate their dinner and turned in a few hours later. Little did they know that they were about to have a nightmare—a *real* nightmare.

Between one and two o'clock in the morning, both men suddenly woke up. Their tent was shaking. "Someone's playing a practical joke," they thought. But the "joke" didn't stop. The poles rattled. The tent collapsed. Then a clawed paw reached through an opening and pulled Roger, screaming, out of the tent.

Ted quickly got up and went outside. The moonlight revealed the outline of a *grizzly bear* towering over Roger, who was motionless on the ground.

The giant grizzly looked up and saw Ted. It quickly grabbed Roger by an ankle and dragged him 30 feet away. Ted hurled a tent pole after the bear and screamed. The bear backed off.

Roger was still alive, but he was badly mauled.

"I'll be right back," said Ted. He ran to the collapsed tent and searched for his glasses and a flash-light.

All of a sudden, his friend screamed. Ted rushed back to the scene. But his buddy was gone. And there was no trace of the bear.

A search party followed a bloody trail into the woods. Two hours later, Roger was discovered. The bear had dragged him more than 200 feet and had eaten parts of his body. Rangers later found—and killed—the bear.

No one was at fault for the attack. The men had followed all the park rules for cooking food in grizzly bear country. They didn't leave food outside, near the tent, and they didn't tease or provoke the bear.

The bear had simply wandered into the campground, looking for food. When it checked out the tent, its paws felt something solid pressed against the walls. Instinct and experience told it to bite. Then the smell of blood triggered it to kill and eat its helpless prey.

"The incredible thing," one expert said, "is not that it happened, but that it doesn't happen more often."

Campers and bears have shared national parks for more than 120 years. (Yellowstone, the first national park in the United States, was created in 1872.) Grizzly bears are under protection from human hunters in Yellowstone and Glacier national parks because they are endangered.

Grizzlies are a type of *brown bear*. They got that name because the whitish tips of their fur give them a grayish, or grizzled, appearance. They live in the western part of North America (Idaho, Montana, Washington, and Wyoming) and in parts of Europe and Asia. They live in caves, rocky crevices, hollow logs, or dense thickets. The average grizzly is 8 feet tall and weighs 790 pounds.

Adult male grizzlies begin to stir and emerge from their winter sleep in late March. They are the first of the grizzlies to greet the spring. Later, the mothers emerge from winter quarters with tiny cubs born in late January and early February. (Bears don't truly *hibernate* in winter. They just sleep a lot. On warm winter days, they're up and about as usual. To hibernate, the body temperature must decrease and most of their bodily functions must stop.)

Mating season for grizzlies is June and early July. The breeding season is the only time males associate with females. Males wander the countryside, parks, or wherever they live in a constant search for food. They need to regain weight lost during their slow, inactive winter.

The average bear—whether it be *black,* brown, or *polar*—keeps away from humans. But some park bears—both black and brown bears—meet so many people that they lose their natural fear. They quickly learn that campers leave behind food. So they *forage,* or search for food, in areas populated by humans, picking through garbage at night while people are sleeping.

Grizzlies forage in campsites, too. They are the most aggressive kind of bear, and the most likely to attack humans. But reported deaths by grizzly bears number less than fifty between 1900 and 1980. American black bears killed half that number during those eighty years. In fact, nine out of ten black bear attacks caused only minor injuries. Polar bears, which live in the Arctic, have caused even fewer human deaths. Even so, they have the same "killer instincts" of all predators.

These killer instincts may explain a tragic event late one night in May of 1987. Juan Perez, 11, jumped a high spiked fence at the Prospect Park Zoo in Brooklyn, New York, on a dare from his friends. Juan waded into the moat of the polar bear cage. The bears were well-fed. They were used to people—zookeepers and visitors alike. But they probably didn't expect to see a strange, small human in their cage so late at night. Two of the bears mauled Juan Perez to death.

The most dangerous bears to watch out for may be mothers. Grizzly mothers are especially tough. They'll charge any human that wanders too close. And their idea of "close" may be quite different from yours—as far away as several hundred yards. Of course, they're not looking for food. They just want to protect their cubs.

Mighty Snackers

Bears may be big, strong predators. But they do eat things other than large prey, including insects, fish, rodents, leaves and herbs, roots, fruit, and nuts.

These mighty killers sometimes even eat tiny ants! From spring to fall, eating takes up much of their time. They need to fatten up for their long winter sleep.

Bears roam for miles—almost anywhere—in search of a meal. They dig up roots in a forest with their long, sharp claws. They chase after mice or squirrels in a field. They wade into streams and use their jaws and paws to catch fish. Some climb trees in pursuit of prey, then drag it down to the ground to eat.

Believe it or not, bears can attack cubs of their own kind. They do it when they're hungry and don't particularly care what they eat. The need to fight off hungry males is one of the main reasons why females get irritated and defensive when they feel their cubs are threatened.

To catch prey, polar bears even "make like snakes," slithering across the Arctic snow. They sneak up on seals sitting on ice floes. Only their small black noses against the white snow gives them away!

Hunting and gathering isn't the only way bears find food. Sometimes, bears claim a dead animal that they find unexpectedly. They defend the meat fiercely, as if it were their own kill.

Smellers Supreme

Whatever food they're after, bears have to find it to eat it. Most species don't see or hear very well. Some may even be *nearsighted,* unable to see far away. But in general, bears have an amazing sense of smell.

A Native American saying goes like this: "A pine needle fell. The eagle saw it. The deer heard it. The bear smelled it."

Most bears can also detect odors left behind on

rocks, trees, and in footprints. One scientist touched a rock, and then watched a brown bear from another spot. The bear ran away as soon as it got a whiff of the leftover scent on the rock!

When grizzlies spot their prey (or a human) nearby, they will usually stand on their hind legs to try to catch a whiff of the target's odor. This does not always mean that they will attack. It is the bear's way of sizing up the situation.

And they may circle an animal to get downwind. (You can only smell something if the wind carries the odor to your nose.)

Once bears get a whiff of something tasty, they sometimes ambush it. They may even stalk it. But much of the time, they just outrun it and overtake it.

Think you could outrun a bear? Think again! An angry grizzly can run at least 30 miles per hour. Plus, unlike lions and tigers, bears have the stamina of a marathon runner. A scientist once tracked a running bear for nearly 10 miles!

Even more scary, big bears can barrel through thick brush that would stop you cold. Their size gives them added *momentum,* the power of a moving object, to mow down things that stand in their way.

The biggest grizzlies can weigh over 850 pounds and grow 8 feet tall. That's heavier than two pro football players and more than a foot taller than most basketball players. *Kodiak bears,* a type of brown bear that lives in Alaska, are the world's largest land predator—they can weigh as much as 1,700 pounds!

With size often comes strength. Grizzlies have turned over rocks weighing hundreds of pounds to get at the tiny insects underneath. And some people have reported grizzlies bending gun barrels! No wonder their Latin scientific name is *Ursus horribilis!*

"Horrible" to us, maybe. But like all meat-eaters, these killers are just doing what comes naturally.

The smell of blood is especially attractive to a shark. Here, a great white shark is drawn out of the water with fresh meat so researchers can study its method of attack.

The lazy and sluggish saltwater crocodile spends many hours sunning itself, perhaps saving energy for a surprise attack on its next victim.

In the past few centuries, there have been fewer than 100 attacks by mountain lions on humans.

The leopard, like all big cats, uses its canine teeth for killing its prey quickly.

A male lion is easily identified by its big fluffy mane. Though the female lion does the hunting, the male eats his share of the kill first.

A Bengal tiger likes to surprise its prey. It won't attack a human or an animal that knows the tiger is there.

American black bears are not as aggressive as other bears. Attacks by black bears usually result in only minor injuries.

The grizzly bear's massive claws can tear the flesh of its prey with one easy swipe.

An angry grizzly bear can run on all fours at a speed of 30 miles per hour.

Polar bears have the same "killer instinct" as other aggressive bears, but they have caused fewer human deaths. This may be because the Arctic regions are sparsely populated.

The piranha is less than a foot long. Most humans who wade into piranha-infested waters in South America manage to escape by jumping out of the water after the first few bites.

Stories and legends have made wild Australian dogs called dingoes out to be fierce man-eaters. The truth is, they almost never attack humans.

5

Man-Eater Myths and Maybes

Many animals that eat meat *could* eat a human being, but don't do it often, or at all.

Take the much-feared *piranha*. This South American fish is less than a foot long, but it has razor-sharp teeth that slice huge chunks out of living flesh. Schools of piranhas—from dozens to thousands—can reduce a large mammal to a skeleton in minutes. What happens if that large mammal is a human?

Deaths by piranha *have* been reported, but they're very rare. Usually, attacks by these tiny "jaws of the Amazon" amount to a few nasty bites. Then the human simply jumps out of the water—fast! And if the person is alone and *can't* escape? The piranhas would treat the victim like any other meal—they would eat him or her.

What other meat-eaters have the ability to hunt humans? Besides piranhas, add the following predators to the "maybe" list of man-eaters.

The *great barracuda,* like man-eating sharks and piranhas, has the weapons to kill humans. Its huge mouth is full of sharp teeth. Plus, it's a very aggressive fish that can grow bigger than a human—about

8 feet long. Scientist Donald de Sylva studied several dozen reported attacks by great barracudas all around the world. Many took place in knee-deep water. And the victims typically lost limbs and died of shock and blood loss.

But were the attackers actually great barracudas? Or sharks? In most cases, it is impossible to tell for sure. Both sharks and barracudas have similar attack patterns. They go after any prey—even humans —that's thrashing around or bleeding or both. Victims that thrash around may be wounded, excited, or fleeing from a predator.

Killer whales are also able to eat humans. These black-and-white colored predators are actually large dolphins. (Whales, dolphins, and porpoises are mammals, not fish.) Killer whales grow up to 30 feet long —about the length of a school bus. They weigh up to 10 tons and have between forty and forty-eight teeth. These animals have big appetites. One killer whale was found to have twenty-eight seals in its stomach!

But do killer whales kill humans? Most of the reported attacks have happened in Antarctica. (Killer whales prefer cold water.) There, the giant mammals hunt seals and penguins sitting on floating ice. A human sitting on floating ice looks similar, so it's possible that some of these reported attacks are true. But in most cases, the evidence suggests that great white sharks—and not killer whales—are the real killers.

Fright of the Reptiles

Saltwater and Nile crocodiles are proven man-eaters. But what about their cousin, the *American alli-*

gator? This big-jawed reptile, the kind found in Florida, is definitely dangerous. It will attack if it feels threatened. But in general, alligators don't have a taste for human flesh. They're much more likely to snap up a pet dog or cat than its owner.

The same goes for the *American crocodile* and other species of crocodiles. They're less aggressive than the salties and the Nile crocodiles.

How do you tell alligators and crocodiles apart? Alligators have wider snouts and more teeth than crocodiles. When their mouths are closed, you can't see their teeth. Crocodiles always have their teeth on display—mouth open or closed. Their teeth have a fang-like appearance because the crocodile's fourth tooth fits into a groove in the side of the upper jaw and is visible when its jaws are closed. In the alligator, this tooth is not visible.

What about other giant reptiles—*anacondas, boa constrictors,* and *pythons?* These huge snakes are all considered constrictors because of how they kill prey. Take the biggest of these snakes, the anaconda. It lives in South American waters. And it can grow 35 feet long—and probably longer! When an anaconda senses nearby prey, it may bite down with curved teeth and a strong jaw. Then the snake coils its long body around the victim. Each time the target lets out a breath, the anaconda squeezes a little tighter. Within minutes, the victim stops struggling, passes out, and *suffocates,* or dies from lack of air.

Could these snakes suffocate—and swallow—a human? Again, the answer is "maybe." People have claimed that their children were killed by snakes, and some of these accidents may have actually happened. But there isn't any hard evidence, so it's difficult to be sure. The odds are that these snakes were simply defending themselves against what they thought were intruders.

Wolves and Scavengers

Wolves and *dingoes* (wild Australian dogs) are hunters and carnivores. Books, movies, and stories have made them out to be feared man-eaters. But the truth is, they almost never attack humans.

On August 17, 1980, in Australia, Lindy Chamberlain claimed that a dingo snapped up her sleeping baby daughter from a campsite. She said it dragged away little Azaria before anyone could rescue her. Dingo attacks are very rare, and that may be one reason Lindy was accused of making up the story. She went on trial for the murder of her baby and even spent time in jail. But evidence later proved that a dingo *had* taken Azaria—and that Lindy was innocent. Azaria's bloody clothes with teeth marks were found in the Australian outback. The movie *A Cry in the Dark* tells about this terrible accident.

Wolf expert C. D. H. Clark collected all the reports of wolf attacks he could find. His conclusion? A few wolf victims—mainly children—died in Europe and Asia in the past few centuries. In many of the cases, the wolf had a disease called *rabies*. (This disease causes animals to act strangely and aggressively.) And some of the wolves *did* eat the human flesh. In North America, however, no human has ever been known to die in the jaws of a healthy wolf. In fact, healthy wolves flee from humans. They're more afraid of us than we are of them!

Another group of meat-eaters are the scavengers. Feeding on the remains or carcasses of others' kills is called scavenging. This group includes any animal that dines on dead flesh—bears, vultures, coyotes, hyenas, and many others. Except for bears, most scavengers aren't big and strong enough to hunt humans—but if the human happens to be already dead and is out in the open. . . . As noted earlier, humans are animals. And all animals are basically living or dead meat. So scavengers would almost certainly make a meal of a dead human, given the chance.

You may be surprised to discover that one of the biggest eaters of dead human flesh is the smallest of creatures—bacteria! *Bacteria* are one-celled organisms. Microscopic bacteria *decompose,* or break down, flesh. So technically they belong on the man-eating list.

A Bad Rap

Just because an animal is big, tough, and well-equipped with "killer" tools doesn't mean it's a man-eater. Or even a meat-eater. Some animals that look ferocious simply have a bad reputation. They wouldn't eat humans if their lives depended on it.

Mountain gorillas, for example, have gotten a bad rap. They are not at all like King Kong! They do have large canines for ripping and tearing flesh, and their sheer size can easily overpower any human. But these weapons are used strictly for self-defense—against other gorillas, mainly. Giant apes are *herbivores,* or plant-eating animals. They prefer soft leaves over flesh.

Elephants, rhinos, and *hippos* also aren't people-eaters. They're all huge and powerful, and sometimes they're dangerous to humans. But they never attack us for food.

One scientist wrote about how he survived a rare charge by a rhino. As the horned beast ran toward him, he jumped behind the nearest bushes. The few branches and twigs offered no defense against this living bulldozer. So the scientist prepared himself for the worst. Then, bam! The rhino stopped dead in its tracks. Its horn was just a foot or so from the terrified scientist. Then it turned around and trotted away! It had no interest in killing, let alone eating, the scientist. The rhino was probably just protecting its territory.

6

Staying Alive

How can you stay safe from meat-eating animals? If you don't want to be their dinner, don't act like their usual prey. Splashing wildly leads a shark to believe you're wounded—an easy meal. Sprinting can trigger the "chase and kill" instinct of a lion. Not watching where you're wading in crocodile-infested waters is an invitation to an ambush.

All predators tune in to the smells, sounds, and actions of their targets. The trick is to fool a killer into backing off. To do that, consider why an animal might attack a human in the first place.

• **You've cornered it.** So it has one choice: Fend for its life. Always give a wild animal an exit.

• **You're a threat.** Just your being there and being unfamiliar can put a wild animal into a self-defense mode.

• **It has babies to protect.** Never mess with a mother—no matter what the species. Mother grizzly bears will give up their own lives to save their cubs.

• **You're in its territory.** So get out. And remember: Predators protect their food supply at all costs.

- **It thinks you're something else.** You may be eating or carrying food that a grizzly finds tasty. Or a shark may mistake you for a seal, take one bite, and then swim away.
- **It's sick, old, or lame.** So it does things it normally wouldn't—namely, go after a human.
- **It's hungry.** The hungrier an animal is, the more risks it will take to fill its empty stomach. Most animals consider attacking humans—the world's fiercest predator—*very* risky. Sharks and crocodiles may not hesitate to attack. The same goes for wild animals that humans have been foolish enough to feed. These animals soon lose their natural fear of humans. Here are a few tips for those rare occasions when you may find yourself in the company of a dangerous predator.

Wade Warily in Water

If you're wading or swimming, predators have a big advantage over you. They're perfectly at home speeding through the water, and you're not. As a land dweller, you feel much more comfortable on solid ground.

So be careful if you swim in waters that may be shark-infested. (This may be difficult to predict, however, because all ocean waters may have sharks in some beach areas, including the eastern Australian Coast and South Africa.) Sharks swim much faster than you do! Though attacks on humans are very, very rare, it pays to keep your eyes wide open. People take shark attacks seriously enough to spend lots of money and brainpower on preventing them. Shark repellents—strong chemicals—work sometimes. But not always.

A sharp knock on the snout with a *billy* (a long stick) can give a swimmer time to get away. But sometimes this can make a shark more aggressive. Live sharks are turned off by rotting shark flesh. (Yet the rotting flesh of other animals is a turn-on.) Metal cages protect shark scientists from their subjects. Nets and electric cables separate swimmers from sharks: Sharks are sensitive to electricity. But the cables are costly and don't always work well.

Follow these simple guidelines for safe swimming:

• **Avoid murky water.** In clear water, you can see—and swim away from—a shark. And the shark can see that you're not its normal prey.

• **Don't swim alone.** Sharks are likely to avoid groups.

• **Don't wear bright, shiny jewelry.** It looks like fish scales. Bright clothing attracts sharks, too. They're especially good at seeing stripes and colors that contrast or are opposite in tone.

• **Don't swim if you're bleeding.** And steer clear of areas where there may be blood—like fishing boats where fish are gutted.

• **If a shark comes near, huddle with other swimmers, facing outward.** The shark can't tell where one human ends and another starts. So it may think you're one huge, tough-to-kill mass.

• **Get out of the water with steady movements.** The same basic advice goes for avoiding crocodiles—avoid muddy waters where crocodiles live. (Bright clothing makes no difference to a croco-dile.) In Australia, the crocodile breeding season is November to April—a time when males become more aggressive. A few more tips:

• **Don't feed wild animals—especially croco-diles!** Crocodiles soon learn that humans mean food. And they'll bite the hand that feeds them.

• **Don't panic or move.** Quick movements can trigger an attack.

• **Let a watchful crocodile know that you know it's there.** Remember that crocodiles prefer surprise attacks.

• **Crocodiles won't fight unless they can win easily.** So if you're with someone, stick together. Two humans are harder to beat than one. And stand up: Look as big as possible. Crouching down and looking small makes you look like easy prey.

• **If a crocodile does attack, keep in mind that it gets tired quickly.** Struggle hard, and the crocodile may decide the fight isn't worth it. Peta-Lynn Mann, 13, found that out in 1981. A 13-foot saltie clamped onto the arm of a man. And as the crocodile tried to drag the man deeper, Peta-Lynn grabbed his other arm. She was a lot weaker than the crocodile. But she pulled and pulled until the crocodile finally got tired and let go. The tug of war saved the injured man's life.

Beware the Wild

Camping puts you closer to lions, and tigers, and bears. However, they don't always want to be close to you. These beasts usually prefer to avoid humans. But what if a big, four-legged mammal decides differently?

• **Don't tempt it.** Keep food supplies away from your tent. The best place to store them is inside a car.

• **Whistle while you walk.** Big beasts will hear you and probably shy away from the strange noises.

• **Stick to open areas.** Lions and tigers need cover (long grass, trees, rocks) to pull off a sneak attack.

• **Avoid being upwind if you know an animal is near.** The wind can carry your scent for miles.

• **If you spot a predator, stay away.** Don't run up and take pictures.

• **In a group, the active person draws the attack.** If a bear or big cat begins attacking one person, friends can confuse the predator by shouting, moving, and dropping things.

• **Don't stare at a bear who's checking you out.** Talk to it as you slowly back away, so that it knows you're not a threat.

• **If it's nearby and isn't attacking, don't run.** Almost all large animals can outrun you. Stay still and calm.

• **If you meet a female bear with cubs, play dead.** Lie facedown, with your arms protecting your head. The mother probably won't attack if you do.

Neighborhood No-No's

Just when you thought it was safe to walk in your own neighborhood . . .

People report about 2 million animal bites each year. Kids are the most common victims. And pet dogs—by far—do most of the biting. Collies, German shepherds, cocker spaniels, Saint Bernards, Great Danes, and pit bulls head the list. Male dogs attack more often than females. And young dogs—less than 4 years old—bite more than older dogs.

Dog and cat bites are almost never fatal. And these animals aren't out to eat you—they're usually just defending themselves. Still, it's a good idea to avoid any kind of attack. Here's how:

• **Pets usually bite people they know.** And these people are usually in the animal's yard or home. Don't challenge a dog or cat on its own ground. Don't taunt it, tease it, or throw things at it.

• **Since dogs and cats aren't stalking you for food, they'll warn you first.** Cats snarl, growl, and lay their ears back. Dogs growl or bark. Take them seriously and back off.

• **If you do get bit, get to a doctor quickly.** Half of all cat bites infect people with harmful germs. And some dogs have a disease called rabies.

Animals that attack humans don't "hate" people. They don't seek revenge. And they don't do it to cause trouble. They're just programmed that way. They defend themselves, defend their young, and kill prey to eat. And sometimes, humans cross their paths without meaning to.

Even after surviving her crocodile attack, Val Plumwood thinks humans should learn to live with all animals. "The world is not just a place for human beings," she says. "It's a crocodile world, too. That goes for other less-than-popular creatures as well. . . . I would have gladly shot the crocodile during the attack. And I don't *like* crocodiles. . . . But they're entitled to their life and their piece of habitat."

Aren't all animals?